# Monsieur de Pourceaugnac by Molière

**Translated by Charles Heron Wall**

Jean-Baptiste Poquelin is better known to us by his stage name of Molière. He was born in Paris, to a prosperous well-to-do family on 15th January 1622.

In 1631, his father purchased from the court of Louis XIII the posts of "valet of the King's chamber and keeper of carpets and upholstery" which Molière assumed in 1641. The benefits included only three months' work per annum for which he was paid 300 livres and also provided a number of lucrative contracts.

However in June 1643, at 21, Molière abandoned this for his first love; a career on the stage. He partnered with the actress Madeleine Béjart, to found the Illustre Théâtre at a cost of 630 livres. Unfortunately despite their enthusiasm, effort and ambition the troupe went bankrupt in 1645.

Molière and Madeleine now began again and spent the next dozen years touring the provincial circuit. His journey back to the sacred land of Parisian theatres was slow but by 1658 he performed in front of the King at the Louvre.

From this point Molière both wrote and acted in a large number of productions that caused both outrage and applause. His many attacks on social conventions, the church, hypocrisy and other areas whilst also writing a large number of comedies, farces, tragicomedies, comédie-ballets are the stuff of legend.

'Tartuffe', 'The Misanthrope', 'The Miser' and 'The School for Wives' are but some of his classics.

His death was as dramatic as his life. Molière suffered from pulmonary tuberculosis. One evening he collapsed on stage in a fit of coughing and haemorrhaging while performing in the last play he'd written, in which, ironically, he was playing the hypochondriac Argan, in 'The Imaginary Invalid'.

Molière insisted on completing his performance.

Afterwards he collapsed again with another, larger haemorrhage and was taken home. Priests were sent for to administer the last rites. Two priests refused to visit. A third arrived too late. On 17th February 1673, Jean-Baptiste Poquelin, forever to be known as Molière, was pronounced dead in Paris. He was 51.

## Index of Contents

NOTES

'Monsieur de Pourceaugnac', acted on October 6, 1669, is nothing but a farce. But Molière excels in farce as well as in higher comedy, and 'Monsieur de Pourceaugnac' is one of the best of its kind. The attacks upon the doctors of the time are not exaggerated. Molière acted the part of Mr. de Pourceaugnac.

DRAMATIS PERSONAE
MR. DE POURCEAUGNAC
ORONTE, father to JULIA
ÉRASTE, lover to JULIA
SBRIGANI, a Neapolitan adventurer
FIRST PHYSICIAN
SECOND PHYSICIAN
AN APOTHECARY
A PEASANT
A FEMALE PEASANT
FIRST SWISS
SECOND SWISS
A POLICE OFFICER
TWO INFERIOR POLICE OFFICERS
JULIA, daughter to ORONTE
NÉRINE, an intriguing woman, supposed to come from Picardy
LUCETTE, supposed to come from Gascony

SCENE: Paris

MR. DE POURCEAUGNAC

ACT I

SCENE I

**ÉRASTE, A LADY SINGER, TWO MEN SINGERS**, several others performing on instruments, **DANCERS**.

**ÉRASTE** [To the **MUSICIANS** and **DANCERS**]
Carry out the orders I have given you for the serenade. As for myself, I will withdraw, for I do not wish to be seen here.

SCENE II

**A LADY SINGER, TWO MEN SINGERS**, several others performing on instruments, **DANCERS**.

**LADY** [Sings]
Spread, charming night, spread over every brow
The subtle scent of thy narcotic flower,
And let no wakeful hearts keep vigil now
Save those enthralled by love's resistless power.
More beautiful than day's most beauteous light,
Thy silent shades were made for love's delight.

**FIRST SINGER**
Love is sweet when none our wills oppose;
Then peaceful tastes our gentle hearts dispose;
But tyrants reign, who gave us birth and life.
Ah! love is sweet when love is free from strife.

**SECOND SINGER**
All who strive 'gainst love must fall;
Perfect love will conquer all.

**ALL THREE**
Let us love with an eternal ardour!
Let parents frown, and try in vain to cure,
Absence, hardship, or cruel fortune's rigour
Will only strengthen love when true and pure.

First entry of the **BALLET**.

[Dance of the two **DANCING MASTERS**.

Second entry of the **BALLET**.

[Dance of the two **PAGES**.

Third entry of the **BALLET**.

[Four **SPECTATORS**, who quarrelled during the dance, now dance, sword in hand, fighting all the while.

Fourth entry of the **BALLET**.

[Two **SOLDIERS** separate the combatants, and dance with them.

SCENE III

**JULIA, ÉRASTE, NÉRINE**.

**JULIA**

Oh dear, Éraste! take care that we are not discovered. I am so afraid of being seen with you; all would be lost after the command I have received to the contrary.

**ÉRASTE**
I see nobody about.

**JULIA** [To **NÉRINE**]
Just keep watch, Nérine, and be careful that nobody comes.

**NÉRINE** [Going to the farther end of the stage]
Trust me for that: and say all you have to say to each other.

**JULIA**
Have you thought of anything to favour our plan, Éraste? And do you think that we shall succeed in breaking off that marriage which my father has taken into his head?

**ÉRASTE**
We are at least doing all we can for it, and we have ready many schemes to bring such an absurd notion to naught.

**NÉRINE** [Running towards **JULIA**]
I say, here is your father.

**JULIA**
Ah! let us separate quickly.

**NÉRINE**
No, no; don't go; I made a mistake.

**JULIA**
How absurd you are, Nérine, to give us such a fright!

**ÉRASTE**
Yes, dear Julia, we have plenty of stratagems ready for the purpose; and, in accordance with the permission you have given me, we will not hesitate to make use of every means. Do not ask me what it is we are going to do; you will have the fun of seeing it, and, as at a comedy, it will be nice for you to have the pleasure of being surprised without my letting you know beforehand what is going to take place. This is telling you that we have many schemes in hand for the occasion, and that our clever Nérine and the dexterous Sbrigani have undertaken to bring the affair to a successful issue.

**NÉRINE**
Yes, we have indeed. Is your father crazy to think of entangling you with his lawyer of Limoges; that Mr. de Pourceaugnac, whom he has never seen in his life, and who comes by the coach to take you away before our very eyes? Ought three or four thousand crowns, more or less—and that, too, upon the word of your uncle—to make him refuse a lover you like? Besides, are you made for a Limousin? If he has taken it into his head to marry, why does he not take one of his own countrywomen, and let Christians be at peace? The very name of Pourceaugnac puts me in a frightful rage. I boil over with Mr. de Pourceaugnac. If it were only because of the name, I would do anything to prevent the match. No, you

shall not be Mrs. de Pourceaugnac. Pourceaugnac! Was ever such a name heard of![1] No, I could never put up with Pourceaugnac; and we will abuse the man to such an extent, and play him so many tricks, that he will have to return to Limoges, Mr. de Pourceaugnac.

**ÉRASTE**
Here is our cunning Neapolitan, who will give us news.


### SCENE IV

**JULIA, ÉRASTE, SBRIGANI, NÉRINE.**

**SBRIGANI**
Our man has just come, Sir. I saw him at a place three leagues away from here, where the coach stops; and I studied him for more than half an hour in the kitchen, where he went down to breakfast, and I know him now perfectly. As to his appearance, I will say nothing about it; you will see for yourselves what nature has done for him, and if his dress is not the very thing to set that off. But as for his understanding, I can tell you beforehand that it is among the dullest I have met with for a long time. We shall find in him a fit subject to work upon as we like. He is just the man to fall into all the traps laid for him.

**ÉRASTE**
Is all that possible?

**SBRIGANI**
Perfectly true, and I am skilled in the knowledge of men.

**NÉRINE** [Pointing to **SBRIGANI**]
This is a famous man, Madam; and your affair could not be trusted to better hands. He is the hero of the age, for the wonders he has performed. A man who, twenty times in his life, has generously braved the galleys to serve his friends; who, at the peril of his arms and shoulders,[2] knows how to bring to a successful issue the most difficult enterprises; and who is, in short, banished from his country for I don't know how many honourable actions he has generously engaged in.

**SBRIGANI**
I am ashamed to hear the praises with which you honour me, and I could most justly extol the marvellous things you did in your life; I could particularly speak of the glory you acquired when you cheated at play that young nobleman we brought to your house, and won twelve thousand crowns from him; when you handsomely made that false contract which ruined a whole family; when with such greatness of soul you denied all knowledge of the deposit which had been entrusted to you, and so generously gave evidence which hung two innocent people.

**NÉRINE**
These are trifles not worth mentioning, and your praises make me blush.

**SBRIGANI**

Then I will spare your modesty. Let us leave that aside, and speak of our business. To begin with, I will quickly rejoin our countryman, while you, on your side, will see that all the other actors in the comedy are kept in readiness.

**ÉRASTE**
And you, Madam, pray remember your part, that in order to conceal our aim the better, you are to affect to be quite perfectly delighted with your father's resolutions.

**JULIA**
If it only depends on that, things will be sure to succeed.

**ÉRASTE**
But, dear Julia, if everything were to fail?

**JULIA**
I will declare my real inclinations to my father.

**ÉRASTE**
And if he persists in his designs in spite of your inclinations?

**JULIA**
I will threaten to shut myself up in a convent.

**ÉRASTE**
But if, notwithstanding all that, he wished to force you to this marriage?

**JULIA**
Why, what would you have me say?

**ÉRASTE**
What do I want you to say?

**JULIA**
Yes.

**ÉRASTE**
What is said when one loves truly?

**JULIA**
But what?

**ÉRASTE**
That nothing shall force you; that in spite of all your father can do, you promise to be mine.

**JULIA**
Ah me! Éraste, be satisfied with what I do now, and leave the future alone. Do not perplex me in my duty, by speaking of sad expedients to which we may not be obliged to have recourse. Allow me to be led by the course of events.

**ÉRASTE**
Will....

**SBRIGANI**
Sir, here is our man. Be careful.

**NÉRINE**
Ah! what a guy![3]


SCENE V

**MR. DE POURCEAUGNAC, SBRIGANI.**

**MR. DE POURCEAUGNAC** [Turning to the side he came from, and speaking to the people who are following him]
Well, what is it? What is the matter? What do you want? Deuce take this stupid town, and the people who live in it! Nobody can walk a step without meeting a lot of asses staring and laughing like fools at one. You boobies, mind your business; and let folk pass without grinning in their faces. Deuce take me if I don't knock down the first man I see laughing.

**SBRIGANI** [Speaking to the same people]
What are you about? What is the meaning of such conduct? What is it you want? Is it right to make fun like that of strangers who come here?

**MR. DE POURCEAUGNAC**
Here is a man of sense at last.

**SBRIGANI**
What manners! And what is there to laugh at?

**MR. DE POURCEAUGNAC**
Quite right.

**SBRIGANI**
Is there anything ridiculous in this gentleman?

**MR. DE POURCEAUGNAC**
I ask you?

**SBRIGANI**
Is he not like other people?

**MR. DE POURCEAUGNAC**
Am I crooked or hunchbacked?

**SBRIGANI**
Learn to distinguish people.

**MR. DE POURCEAUGNAC**
Well said.

**SBRIGANI**
This gentleman's qualities call for your respect.

**MR. DE POURCEAUGNAC**
Perfectly true.

**SBRIGANI**
He is a person of quality.

**MR. DE POURCEAUGNAC**
Yes, a gentleman from Limoges.

**SBRIGANI**
A man of intelligence.

**MR. DE POURCEAUGNAC**
Who has studied the law.[4]

**SBRIGANI**
He does you too much honour in coming to this town.

**MR. DE POURCEAUGNAC**
Ay, indeed.

**SBRIGANI**
This gentleman has nothing in him that can make you laugh.

**MR. DE POURCEAUGNAC**
Certainly not.

**SBRIGANI**
And the first who laughs at him, I will call to account.

**MR. DE POURCEAUGNAC** [To **SBRIGANI**]
Sir, I am extremely, obliged to you.

**SBRIGANI**
I am sorry, Sir, to see a person like you received after such a fashion.

**MR. DE POURCEAUGNAC**
Your servant, Sir.

**SBRIGANI**
I saw you breakfasting this morning, Sir, with the other passengers; and the grace with which you ate created in me at once a great friendship for you; and as I know that you have never been here before, and that you are a perfect stranger, I am glad I met you, to offer you my services at your arrival, and to assist you among these people, who do not always behave to strangers of quality as they should.

**MR. DE POURCEAUGNAC**
You are really very kind.

**SBRIGANI**
I have told you already; the moment I saw you, I felt an inclination for you.

**MR. DE POURCEAUGNAC**
I am greatly obliged to you.

**SBRIGANI**
Your countenance pleased me.

**MR. DE POURCEAUGNAC**
You do me much honour.

**SBRIGANI**
I read honesty in it.

**MR. DE POURCEAUGNAC**
I am your servant

**SBRIGANI**
Something amiable.

**MR. DE POURCEAUGNAC**
Ah! ah!

**SBRIGANI**
Graceful.

**MR. DE POURCEAUGNAC**
Ah! ah!

**SBRIGANI**
Sweet.

**MR. DE POURCEAUGNAC**
Ah! ah!

**SBRIGANI**
Majestic.

**MR. DE POURCEAUGNAC**
Ah! ah!

**SBRIGANI**
Frank.

**MR. DE POURCEAUGNAC**
Ah! ah!

**SBRIGANI**
And cordial.

**MR. DE POURCEAUGNAC**
Ah! ah!

**SBRIGANI**
Believe that I am entirely yours.

**MR. DE POURCEAUGNAC**
I am greatly obliged to you.

**SBRIGANI**
I speak from the bottom of my heart.

**MR. DE POURCEAUGNAC**
I believe you.

**SBRIGANI**
If I had the honour of being known to you, you would find that I am altogether sincere.

**MR. DE POURCEAUGNAC**
I do not doubt it.

**SBRIGANI**
An enemy to deceit.

**MR. DE POURCEAUGNAC**
I feel sure of it.

**SBRIGANI**
And that I am incapable of disguising my thoughts.

**MR. DE POURCEAUGNAC**
It is exactly what I think.

**SBRIGANI**
You look at my dress, which is not like that of other people; but I came originally from Naples, at your service; and I always like to keep up the way of dressing as well as the sincerity of my country.[5]

**MR. DE POURCEAUGNAC**

You are quite right. For my part, I was desirous of appearing in the court dress for the country.[6]

**SBRIGANI**

Truly, it becomes you better than it does all our courtiers.

**MR. DE POURCEAUGNAC**

Exactly what my tailor told me. The coat is suitable and rich; it will tell here among these people.

**SBRIGANI**

You will go to the Louvre, no doubt?

**MR. DE POURCEAUGNAC**

Yes; I must go and pay my court.

**SBRIGANI**

The king will be charmed to see you.

**MR. DE POURCEAUGNAC**

I believe so.

**SBRIGANI**

Have you fixed upon rooms?

**MR. DE POURCEAUGNAC**

No; I was going to look for some.

**SBRIGANI**

I shall be very glad to go with you; I know all this city well.


SCENE VI

**ÉRASTE, MR. DE POURCEAUGNAC, SBRIGANI.**

**ÉRASTE**

Ah, who is this? What do I see? What a happy meeting! Mr. de Pourceaugnac! How delighted I am to see you! What! anyone would think that you find it difficult to remember me!

**MR. DE POURCEAUGNAC**

Sir, I am your servant.

**ÉRASTE**

Is it possible that five or six years can have made you forget me? Do you not remember the best friend of the de Pourceaugnacs?

**MR. DE POURCEAUGNAC**
Yes, yes.
[Aside to **SBRIGANI**]
Deuce take me if I know who he is.

**ÉRASTE**
There is not one of the de Pourceaugnacs of Limoges that I do not know, from the greatest to the smallest; I visited only them during my stay there, and I had the honour of seeing you every day.

**MR. DE POURCEAUGNAC**
The honour was mine, Sir.

**ÉRASTE**
You do not remember my face?

**MR. DE POURCEAUGNAC**
Yes, yes.
[To **SBRIGANI**]
I don't know him a bit.

**ÉRASTE**
You do not remember that I had the pleasure of drinking with you I don't know how many times?

**MR. DE POURCEAUGNAC**
Excuse me.
[To **SBRIGANI**]
I don't know anything about it.

**ÉRASTE**
What is the name of that pastrycook who cooks such capital dinners?

**MR. DE POURCEAUGNAC**
Petit-Jean.

**ÉRASTE**
Just so. We used often to go there together to enjoy ourselves. How do you call that place where people go for a walk?

**MR. DE POURCEAUGNAC**
The cemetery of the Arènes.

**ÉRASTE**
Exactly. It is there I enjoyed so many happy hours of your pleasant talk. Don't you remember it all now?

**MR. DE POURCEAUGNAC**
Pardon me; yes, I remember.
[To **SBRIGANI**]
Deuce take me if I do.

**SBRIGANI** [Aside to **MR. DE POURCEAUGNAC**]

There are a hundred things like that which one is apt to forget altogether.

**ÉRASTE**

Let us embrace, I pray, and renew our former friendship.

**SBRIGANI** [To **MR. DE POURCEAUGNAC**]

This man seems to have a great affection for you.

**ÉRASTE**

Tell me some news of all the family. How is that gentleman your ... he who is such an honest man?

**MR. DE POURCEAUGNAC**

My brother the sheriff?[7]

**ÉRASTE**

Yes.

**MR. DE POURCEAUGNAC**

He is as well as can be.

**ÉRASTE**

I am delighted to hear it. And that good tempered man? You know, your ...

**MR. DE POURCEAUGNAC**

My cousin, the assessor?

**ÉRASTE**

Exactly.

**MR. DE POURCEAUGNAC**

Always gay and hearty.

**ÉRASTE**

It gives me much pleasure to hear it. And your uncle, the ...

**MR. DE POURCEAUGNAC**

I have no uncle.

**ÉRASTE**

But you had one in those days?

**MR. DE POURCEAUGNAC**

No; only an aunt....

**ÉRASTE**

Ah! it's what I meant; your aunt; Mrs.... How is she?

**MR. DE POURCEAUGNAC**
She died six months ago.

**ÉRASTE**
Alas! poor woman. She was so good, too!

**MR. DE POURCEAUGNAC**
We have also my nephew, the canon, who almost died of the smallpox.

**ÉRASTE**
What a pity if it had happened!

**MR. DE POURCEAUGNAC**
Do you know him also?

**ÉRASTE**
Indeed I do; a tall handsome fellow.

**MR. DE POURCEAUGNAC**
Not so very tall.

**ÉRASTE**
No; but well-shaped.

**MR. DE POURCEAUGNAC**
Yes, yes.

**ÉRASTE**
He's your nephew, isn't he?

**MR. DE POURCEAUGNAC**
Yes.

**ÉRASTE**
Son of your brother or your sister?

**MR. DE POURCEAUGNAC**
True.

**ÉRASTE**
A canon of the church of.... How do you call it?

**MR. DE POURCEAUGNAC**
Saint Stephen.

**ÉRASTE**
Just so; I don't know any other.

**MR. DE POURCEAUGNAC** [To **SBRIGANI**]

He knows all my relations.

**SBRIGANI**

He knows you better than you think.

**MR. DE POURCEAUGNAC**

You must have lived a long time in our town, I see.

**ÉRASTE**

Two whole years.

**MR. DE POURCEAUGNAC**

You were there, then, when our governor was godfather to my cousin the assessor's child?

**ÉRASTE**

To be sure; I was one of the first invited.

**MR. DE POURCEAUGNAC**

The thing was well done.

**ÉRASTE**

Very.

**MR. DE POURCEAUGNAC**

The dinner was well got up.

**ÉRASTE**

Yes, indeed.

**MR. DE POURCEAUGNAC**

Then you must remember the quarrel I had with that gentleman from Périgord.

**ÉRASTE**

Yes.

**MR. DE POURCEAUGNAC**

He met with his match, eh?

**ÉRASTE**

Ah! ah!

**MR. DE POURCEAUGNAC**

He slapped my face; but I paid him back handsomely.

**ÉRASTE**

Very handsomely. By the bye, I shall not allow you to go to any other house but mine.

**MR. DE POURCEAUGNAC**
I would not....

**ÉRASTE**
Nonsense! I will not allow one of my best friends to go anywhere but to my house.

**MR. DE POURCEAUGNAC**
It would be disturb....

**ÉRASTE**
No; deuce take it all. You shall stay with me.

**SBRIGANI** [To **MR. DE POURCEAUGNAC**]
Since he will have it so, I advise you to accept.

**ÉRASTE**
Where is your luggage?

**MR. DE POURCEAUGNAC**
With my servant, where we stopped.

**ÉRASTE**
Send somebody to fetch it.

**MR. DE POURCEAUGNAC**
No. I forbade him to let it go out of his sight, for fear of swindlers.

**SBRIGANI**
You did quite right.

**MR. DE POURCEAUGNAC**
It is good to be cautious in this place.

**ÉRASTE**
We always know a man of sense.

**SBRIGANI**
I will accompany this gentleman, and bring him back where you wish.

**ÉRASTE**
Do so. I have a few orders to give; but you only need come to that house yonder.

**SBRIGANI**
We will come back presently.

**ÉRASTE** [To **MR. DE POURCEAUGNAC**]
I shall expect you with great impatience.

**MR. DE POURCEAUGNAC** [To **SBRIGANI**]

I find an acquaintance when I little expected to meet with one.

**SBRIGANI**

He looks like an honest man.

[Exeunt.

**ÉRASTE** [Alone]

Ah! ah! Mr. de Pourceaugnac, you will get it hot! Everything is ready, and I have only to give the word. Soho! there.

SCENE VII

**ÉRASTE**, AN **APOTHECARY**.

**ÉRASTE**

I think, Sir, that you are the doctor to whom somebody went to speak in my name.

**APOTHECARY**

No, Sir. I am not the doctor; such an honour does not belong to me. I am only an unworthy apothecary; at your service.

**ÉRASTE**

Is the doctor at home, then.

**APOTHECARY**

Yes; he is in there, trying to get rid quickly of some patients. I will tell him that you are here.

**ÉRASTE**

No; you need not disturb him; I will wait till he has done. I have to entrust to his care a certain relation of mine he was told about today. He is attacked with a sort of madness that we should like to see cured before we marry him to anyone.

**APOTHECARY**

I know; I know all about it. I was there when he was told of this affair. Upon my word, Sir; upon my word, you could not apply to a more skilful doctor. He is a man who understands medicine thoroughly, as well as I do my A B C;[8] and who, were you to die for it, would not abate one iota of the rules of the ancients. Yes, he always follows the high-road—the high-road, Sir, and doesn't spend his time finding out mares' nests. For all the gold in the world he would not cure anybody with other medicines than those prescribed by the faculty.

**ÉRASTE**

He is quite right. A patient should not wish to be cured unless the faculty consents to it.

**APOTHECARY**

It is not because we are great friends that I speak so of him; but it is a pleasure to be his patient, and I had rather die by his medicines than be cured with those of another. For, whatever may happen, we know for certain that things are always in due order; and should we die under his care, our heirs have nothing to reproach us with.

**ÉRASTE**

A great comfort to a dead man.

**APOTHECARY**

Certainly; it is pleasant to have died according to rules. Moreover, he is not one of those doctors who let a disease off. He is an expeditious man—expeditious, Sir, who likes to clear off his patients; and when they are to die, the thing is done in no time.

**ÉRASTE**

There is, to be sure, nothing like going through the business quickly.

**APOTHECARY**

Indeed, what is the use of haggling over the matter, and beating so long about the bush? One should know offhand the long and short of an illness.

**ÉRASTE**

You are quite right.

**APOTHECARY**

Why, he did me the honour of taking care of three of my children; they died in less than four days, whereas with another they would have lingered for more than three months.

**ÉRASTE**

It is a blessing to have friends like these.

**APOTHECARY**

Decidedly. I have still two children left, of whom he takes care as if they were his own; he attends them, and physics them as he pleases, without my interfering in the least; and very frequently on my return from the city, I am quite surprised to find that they have been bled or purged by his direction.

**ÉRASTE**

This is kind care indeed!

**APOTHECARY**

Here he is, here he is; here he is coming.


SCENE VIII

**ÉRASTE, 1ST PHYSICIAN, APOTHECARY, COUNTRYMAN, COUNTRYWOMAN.**

**COUNTRYMAN**

Sir, he can hold out no longer; he says he feels the greatest pains imaginable in his head.

**1ST PHYSICIAN**

The patient is a fool; for in the disease by which he is attacked it is not his head, according to Galen, but the spleen, which must give pain.

**COUNTRYMAN**

However this may be, Sir, he has had for the last six months a laxity with it.

**1ST PHYSICIAN**

That's right. It is a sign that his body is clearing. I will go and see him in two or three days; but if he dies before, mind you do not forget to give me notice, for it is not proper that a doctor should go to visit a dead man.

**COUNTRYWOMAN** [To1ST PHYSICIAN]

My father, Sir, is getting worse and worse.

**1ST PHYSICIAN**

It is no fault of mine; I send him remedies; why does he not get better? How many times has he been bled?

**COUNTRYWOMAN**

Fifteen times, Sir, in twenty days.

**1ST PHYSICIAN**

Fifteen times?

**COUNTRYWOMAN**

Yes.

**1ST PHYSICIAN**

And he does not get better?

**COUNTRYWOMAN**

No, Sir.

**1ST PHYSICIAN**

It is a sign that the seat of the malady is not in the blood. He must be purged as many times, to see if it is in the humours; and if this does not succeed, we will send him to the bath.

**APOTHECARY**

This is the beau-idéal of physic.

SCENE IX

**ÉRASTE, 1ST PHYSICIAN, APOTHECARY.**

**ÉRASTE** [To the **1ST PHYSICIAN**]
It was I, Sir, who sent to you few days ago about a relation of mine who is not quite right in his mind; and I want him to live in your house, as it would be more convenient for you to attend to him, and to prevent him from being seen by too many people.

**1ST PHYSICIAN**
Yes, Sir, I have got everything ready; and I will take the utmost care of him.

**ÉRASTE**
Here he is.

**1ST PHYSICIAN**
That is most fortunate; for I have with me just now an old physician, a friend of mine, with whom I should be glad to consult concerning this disorder.

SCENE X

**MR. DE POURCEAUGNAC, ÉRASTE, 1ST PHYSICIAN, APOTHECARY.**

**ÉRASTE** [To **MR. DE POURCEAUGNAC**]
I am obliged to leave you a moment for a little affair which requires my presence;

[Showing the **PHYSICIAN**.

—but this person, in whose hands I leave you, will do for you all he possibly can.

**1ST PHYSICIAN**
I am bound by my profession to do so; and it is enough that you should lay this duty upon me.

**MR. DE POURCEAUGNAC** [Aside]
It is his steward, no doubt; he must be a man of quality.

**1ST PHYSICIAN** [To **ÉRASTE**]
Yes, Sir; I assure you that I shall treat this gentleman methodically, and in strict accordance with the rules of our art.

**MR. DE POURCEAUGNAC**
Indeed, I do not ask for so much ceremony; and I have not come here to trouble you so.

**1ST PHYSICIAN**
Such a duty is a pleasure to me.

**ÉRASTE** [To **1ST PHYSICIAN**]
Nevertheless, here are ten pistoles beforehand, as an earnest of what I have promised you.

**MR. DE POURCEAUGNAC**

No, if you please; I won't hear of your spending anything on my account, nor do I wish you to send for anything particular for me.

**ÉRASTE**

Ah, pray, do not trouble yourself; it is not for that you imagine.

**MR. DE POURCEAUGNAC**

I beg of you to treat me only as a friend.

**ÉRASTE**

It is exactly what I mean to do.
[Aside to the **PHYSICIAN**]
I particularly recommend you not to let him slip out of your hands, for at times he tries to escape.

**1ST PHYSICIAN**

You need not fear.

**ÉRASTE** [To **MR. DE POURCEAUGNAC**]

Pray excuse the incivility I commit.

**MR. DE POURCEAUGNAC**

Don't mention it. You are really too kind.


SCENE XI

**MR. DE POURCEAUGNAC, 1ST PHYSICIAN, 2ND PHYSICIAN, APOTHECARY.**

**1ST PHYSICIAN**

It is a great honour to me to be chosen to do you a service.

**MR. DE POURCEAUGNAC**

I am your servant.

**1ST PHYSICIAN**

Here is a clever man, one of my brethren, with whom I will consult concerning the manner of our treating you.

**MR. DE POURCEAUGNAC**

There is no need of so much ceremony, I tell you; I am easily satisfied.

**1ST PHYSICIAN**

Bring some seats.

[**SERVANTS** come in and place chairs.

**MR. DE POURCEAUGNAC** [Aside]
These servants are rather dismal for a young man.

**1ST PHYSICIAN**
Now, Sir; take a seat, Sir.

[The two **PHYSICIANS** make **MR. DE POURCEAUGNAC** sit between them.

**MR. DE POURCEAUGNAC** [Seated]
Your very humble servant.

[Each **PHYSICIAN** takes one of his hands, and feels his pulse.) What are you about?

**1ST PHYSICIAN**
Do you eat well, Sir?

**MR. DE POURCEAUGNAC**
Yes; and drink still better.

**1ST PHYSICIAN**
So much the worse! That great craving for cold and wet is a sign of the heat and aridity that is within. Do you sleep well?

**MR. DE POURCEAUGNAC**
Yes; when I have made a hearty supper.

**1ST PHYSICIAN**
Do you dream much?

**MR. DE POURCEAUGNAC**
Now and then.

**1ST PHYSICIAN**
Of what nature are your dreams?

**MR. DE POURCEAUGNAC**
Of the nature of dreams. What the deuce is the meaning of this conversation?

**1ST PHYSICIAN**
Have a little patience. We will reason upon your affair in your presence; and we will do it in the vulgar tongue, so that you may understand better.

**MR. DE POURCEAUGNAC**
What great reasoning is there wanted to eat a mouthful?

**1ST PHYSICIAN**

Since it is a fact that we cannot cure any disease without first knowing it perfectly, and that we cannot know it perfectly without first establishing its exact nature and its true species by its diagnosis and prognosis, you will give me leave, you, my senior, to enter upon the consideration of the disease that is in question, before we think of the therapeutics and the remedies that we must decide upon in order to effect a perfect cure. I say then, Sir, if you will allow me, that our patient here present is unhappily attacked, affected, possessed, and disordered by that kind of madness which we properly name hypochondriac melancholy; a very trying kind of madness, and which requires no less than an Aesculapius deeply versed in our art like you; you, I say, who have become grey in harness, as the saying hath it; and through whose hands so much business of all sorts has passed. I call it hypochondriac melancholy, to distinguish it from the other two; for the celebrated Galen establishes and decides in a most learned manner, as is usual with him, that there are three species of the disease which we call melancholy, so called, not only by the Latins, but also by the Greeks; which in this case is worthy of remark: the first, which arises from a direct disease of the brain; the second, which proceeds from the whole of the blood, made and rendered atrabilious; and the third, termed hypochondriac, which is our case here, and which proceeds from some lower part of the abdomen; and from the inferior regions, but particularly the spleen; the heat and inflammation whereof sends up to the brain of our patient abundance of thick and foul fuliginosities; of which the black and gross vapours cause deterioration to the functions of the principal faculty, and cause the disease by which he is manifestly accused and convicted. In proof of what I say, and as an incontestable diagnostic of it, you need only consider that great seriousness, that sadness, accompanied by signs of fearfulness and suspicion—pathognomonic and particular symptoms of this disease, so well defined by the divine ancient Hippocrates; that countenance, those red and staring eyes, that long beard, that habit of body, thin, emaciated, black, and hairy—signs denoting him greatly affected by the disease proceeding from a defect in the hypochondria; which disease, by lapse of time, being naturalised, chronic, habitual, ingrained, and established within him, might well degenerate either into monomania, or into phthisis, or into apoplexy, or even into downright frenzy and raving. All this being taken for granted, since a disease well-known is a disease half cured, for ignoti nulla est curatio morbis, it will not be difficult for you to conclude what are the remedies needed by our patient. First of all, to remedy this obdurate plethora, and this luxuriant cacochymy throughout the body, I opine that he should be freely phlebotomised; by which I mean that there should be frequent and abundant bleedings, first in the basilic vein, then in the cephalic vein; and if the disease be obstinate, that even the vein of the forehead should be opened, and that the orifice be large, so that the thick blood may issue out; and, at the same time, that he should be purged, deobstructed, and evacuated by fit and suitable purgatives, i.e. by chologues and melanogogues. And as the real source of all this mischief is either a foul and feculent humour or a black and gross vapour, which obscures, empoisons, and contaminates the animal spirits, it is proper afterwards that he should have a bath of pure and clean water, with abundance of whey; to purify, by the water, the feculency of the foul humour, and by the whey to clarify the blackness of the vapour. But, before all things, I think it desirable to enliven him by pleasant conversations, by vocal and instrumental music, to which it will not be amiss to add dancers, that their movements, figures, and agility may stir up and awaken the sluggishness of his spirits, which occasions the thickness of his blood from whence the disease proceeds. These are the remedies I propose, to which may be added many better ones by you, Sir, my master and senior, according to the experience, judgment, knowledge and sufficiency that you have acquired in our art. Dixi.

## 2ND PHYSICIAN

Heaven forbid, Sir, that it should enter my thoughts to add anything to what you have just been saying! You have discoursed too well on all the signs, symptoms, and causes of this gentleman's disease. The arguments you have used are so learned and so delicate that it is impossible for him not to be mad and hypochondriacally melancholic; or, were he not, that he ought to become so, because of the beauty of the things you have spoken, and of the justness of your reasoning. Yes, Sir, you have graphically depicted, graphice depinxisti, everything that appertains to this disease. Nothing can be more learnedly, judiciously, and ingeniously conceived, thought, imagined, than what you have delivered on the subject of this disease, either as regards the diagnostic, the prognostic, or the therapeutic; and nothing remains for me to do but to congratulate this gentleman upon falling into your hands, and to tell him that he is but too fortunate to be mad, in order to experience the gentle efficacy of the remedies you have so judiciously proposed. I approve them in toto, manibus et pedibus descendo in tuam sententiam. All I should like to add is to let all his bleedings and purgings be of an odd number, numero deus impare gaudet, to take the whey before the bath, and to make him a forehead plaster, in the composition of which there should be salt—salt is a symbol of wisdom; to whitewash the walls of his room, to dissipate the gloominess of his mind; album est disgregativum visas; and to give him a little injection immediately, to serve as a prelude and introduction to those judicious remedies, from which, if he is curable, he must receive relief. Heaven grant that these remedies, which are yours, Sir, may succeed with the patient according to our wish!

**MR. DE POURCEAUGNAC**
Gentlemen, I have been listening to you for the last hour. Are we acting a comedy here?

**1ST PHYSICIAN**
No, Sir; we are not acting a comedy.

**MR. DE POURCEAUGNAC**
What does it all mean? What are you about with this gibberish and nonsense of yours?

**1ST PHYSICIAN**
Ah! Insulting language! A diagnostic which was wanting for the confirmation of his disease. This may turn to mania.

**MR. DE POURCEAUGNAC** [Aside]
With what kind of people have they left me here.

[He spits two or three times.

**1ST PHYSICIAN**
Another diagnostic: frequent expectoration.

**MR. DE POURCEAUGNAC**
Let us cease all this, and go away.

**1ST PHYSICIAN**
Another: anxiety to move about.

**MR. DE POURCEAUGNAC**
What is the meaning of all this business? What do you want with me?

**1ST PHYSICIAN**
To cure you, according to the order we have received.

**MR. DE POURCEAUGNAC**
Cure me?

**1ST PHYSICIAN**
Yes.

**MR. DE POURCEAUGNAC**
S'death! I am not ill.

**1ST PHYSICIAN**
It is a bad sign when a patient does not feel his illness.

**MR. DE POURCEAUGNAC**
I tell you that I am quite well.

**1ST PHYSICIAN**
We know better than you how you are; we are physicians who see plainly into your constitution.

**MR. DE POURCEAUGNAC**
If you are physicians, I have nothing to do with you; and I snap my fingers at all your physic.

**1ST PHYSICIAN**
H'm! h'm! This man is madder than we thought.

**MR. DE POURCEAUGNAC**
My father and mother would never have anything to do with remedies; and they both died without the help of doctors.

**1ST PHYSICIAN**
I do not wonder if they have begotten a son who is mad.
[To the **2ND PHYSICIAN**]
Come, let us begin the cure; and, through the exhilarating sweetness of harmony, let us dulcify, lenify, and pacify the acrimony of his spirits, which, I see, are ready to be inflamed.

[Exeunt.

SCENE XII

**MR. DE POURCEAUGNAC** [Alone]
What the devil is all this? Are the people of this place crazy? I never saw anything like it; and I don't understand it a bit.

SCENE XIII

**MR. DE POURCEAUGNAC, TWO PHYSICIANS**, in grotesque clothes.

[They all three at first sit down; the **PHYSICIANS** rise up at different times to bow to **MR. DE POURCEAUGNAC**, who rises up as often to bow to them in return.

**THE TWO PHYSICIANS**
Buon dì, buon dì, buon dì!
Non vi lasciate uccidere
Dal dolor malinconico.
Noi vi faremo ridere
Col nostro canto armonico;
Sol per guarirvi.
Siamo venuti quì.
Buon dì, buon dì, buon dì!

**1ST PHYSICIAN**
Altro non è la pazzia
Che malinconia.
Il malato
Non è disperato
Se vol pigliar un poco d'allegria,
Altro non è la pazzia
Che malinconia.

**2ND PHYSICIAN**
Sù; cantate, ballate, ridete.
E, se far meglio volete,
Quando sentite il deliro vicino
Pigliate del vino,
E qualche volta un poco di tabàc.
Allegramente, Monsu Pourceaugnàc.[9]

SCENE XIV
**BALLET.**

SCENE XV

**MR. DE POURCEAUGNAC, AN APOTHECARY.**

**APOTHECARY**
Sir, here is a little remedy; a little remedy which you must take, if you please; if you please.

**MR. DE POURCEAUGNAC**

How? I have no occasion for anything of the kind.

**APOTHECARY**
It was ordered, Sir; it was ordered.

**MR. DE POURCEAUGNAC**
Ah! What noise and bother.

**APOTHECARY**
Take it, Sir; take it, Sir. It will do you no harm; it will do you no harm, &c.

[**MR. DE POURCEAUGNAC** runs away, the **APOTHECARY**, &c. after him.

SCENE XVI

**MR. DE POURCEAUGNAC, AN APOTHECARY, TWO PHYSICIANS**, in grotesque clothes.

**THE TWO PHYSICIANS**
Piglialo sù,
Signor Monsu;
Piglialo, piglialo, piglialo sù,
Che non ti fara, male, &c.[10]

ACT II

SCENE I

**1ST PHYSICIAN, SBRIGANI.**

**1ST PHYSICIAN**
He has forced through every obstacle I had placed to hinder him, and has fled from the remedies I was beginning to prepare for him.

**SBRIGANI**
To avoid remedies so salutary as yours is to be a great enemy to oneself.

**1ST PHYSICIAN**
It is the mark of a disturbed brain and of a depraved reason to be unwilling to be cured.

**SBRIGANI**
You would have cured him, for certain, in no time.

**1ST PHYSICIAN**
Certainly; though there had been the complication of a dozen diseases.

**SBRIGANI**
With all that he makes you lose those fifty well-earned pistoles.

**1ST PHYSICIAN**
I have no intention of losing them; and I am determined to cure him in spite of himself. He is bound and engaged to take my remedies; and I will have him seized, wherever I can find him, as a deserter from physic and an infringer of my prescriptions.

**SBRIGANI**
You are right. Your medicines were sure of their effect; and it is so much money he takes from you.

**1ST PHYSICIAN**
Where could I find him?

**SBRIGANI**
No doubt, at the house of that goodman Oronte, whose daughter he comes to marry; and who, knowing nothing of the infirmity of his future son-in-law, will perhaps be in a hurry to conclude the marriage.

**1ST PHYSICIAN**
I will go and speak to him at once.

**SBRIGANI**
You should, in justice to yourself.

**1ST PHYSICIAN**
He is in need of my consultations; and a patient must not make a fool of his doctor.

**SBRIGANI**
That is well said; and, if I were you, I would not suffer him to marry till you have physicked him to your heart's content.

**1ST PHYSICIAN**
Leave that to me.

**SBRIGANI** [Aside, and going]
For my part, I will bring another battery into play; for the father-in-law is as much of a dupe as the son-in-law.


SCENE II

**ORONTE, 1ST PHYSICIAN.**

**1ST PHYSICIAN**
A certain gentleman, Sir, a Mr. de Pourceaugnac, is to marry your daughter; is he not?

**ORONTE**

Yes; I expect him from Limoges, and he ought to have been here before now.

**1ST PHYSICIAN**

And he has come; he has run away from my house, after having been placed under my care; but I forbid you, in the name of the faculty, to proceed with the marriage you have decided upon, before I have duly prepared him for it, and put him in a state to have children well-conditioned both in mind and body.

**ORONTE**

What is it you mean?

**1ST PHYSICIAN**

Your intended son-in-law was entered as my patient. His disease which was given me to cure is a chattel which belongs to me, and which I reckon among my possessions. I therefore declare to you that I will not allow him to marry before he has rendered due satisfaction to the faculty, and submitted to the remedies which I have ordered for him.

**ORONTE**

He is suffering from some disease?

**1ST PHYSICIAN**

Yes.

**ORONTE**

And from what disease, if you please?

**1ST PHYSICIAN**

Don't trouble yourself about that.

**ORONTE**

Is it some disease....?

**1ST PHYSICIAN**

Doctors are bound to keep things secret. Let it suffice you that I enjoin both you and your daughter not to celebrate the wedding without my consent, upon pain of incurring the displeasure of the faculty, and of undergoing all the diseases which we choose to lay upon you.

**ORONTE**

If that is the case, I shall take good care to put a stop to the marriage.

**1ST PHYSICIAN**

He was entrusted to me, and he is bound to be my patient.

**ORONTE**

Very well.

**1ST PHYSICIAN**

It is in vain for him to run away; I will have him sentenced to be cured by me.

**ORONTE**
I am very willing.

**1ST PHYSICIAN**
Yes; he must either die or be cured by me.

**ORONTE**
I consent to it.

**1ST PHYSICIAN**
And if I cannot find him, I will make you answerable, and cure you instead of him.

**ORONTE**
I am in very good health.

**1ST PHYSICIAN**
No matter. I must have a patient, and I will take anyone I can.

**ORONTE**
Take whom you will, but it shall not be me.
[Alone]
Did you ever hear of such a thing!


SCENE III

**ORONTE**, **SBRIGANI** as a Flemish merchant.

**SBRIGANI**
Sir, py your leafe, I pe one voreign marchant, and vould like ask you one littel news.

**ORONTE**
What, Sir?

**SBRIGANI**
Put you de hat on de head, Sir, if you pleace.

**ORONTE**
Tell me. Sir, what you want.

**SBRIGANI**
I tell nozink, Sir, if you not put de hat on de head.

**ORONTE**
Very well, then, what is it, Sir?

**SBRIGANI**
You not know in dis town one Mister Oronte?

**ORONTE**
Yes, I know him.

**SBRIGANI**
And vat for one man is he, Sir, if you pleace?

**ORONTE**
He is like any other man.

**SBRIGANI**
I ask you, Sir, if he one man of money is?

**ORONTE**
Yes.

**SBRIGANI**
But very mooch rich, Sir?

**ORONTE**
Yes.

**SBRIGANI**
It does me mooch pleasure, Sir.

**ORONTE**
But why should it?

**SBRIGANI**
It is, Sir, for one littel great reason for us.

**ORONTE**
But why?

**SBRIGANI**
It is, Sir, dat dis Mr. Oronte his tauchter in marriage to a certain Mr. Pourgnac gifes.

**ORONTE**
Well!

**SBRIGANI**
And dis Mr. Pourgnac, Sir, is one man vat owes mooch golt to ten or twelf Flemish marchants vat come here.

**ORONTE**
This Mr. de Pourceaugnac owes a great deal to ten or twelve merchants?

**SBRIGANI**
Yes, Sir; and for de last eight months ve hafe obtain one littel judgment against him, and he put off all de credeetors till dis marriage vat Mr. Oronte gifes to his tauchter.

**ORONTE**
Ho! ho! So he puts off paying his creditors till then?

**SBRIGANI**
Yes, Sir; and vid great defotion ve all wait for dis marriage.

**ORONTE**
The idea is not bad.
[Aloud]
I wish you good day.

**SBRIGANI**
I tank de gentleman for de favour great.

**ORONTE**
Your very humble servant.

**SBRIGANI**
I pe, Sir, more great obliged don all py de goot news vat the Mister gife me.

[Alone, after having taken off his beard, and taken off the Flemish dress which he has put over his.

Things don't go badly. All is going on swimmingly. I must throw off this disguise and think of something else. We will put so much suspicion between the father-in-law and his son-in-law that the intended marriage must come to nothing. They are both equally fit to swallow the baits that are laid for them, and it is mere child's play for us great sharpers when we find such easy gulls.

SCENE IV

**MR. DE POURCEAUGNAC, SBRIGANI.**

**MR. DE POURCEAUGNAC** [Thinking himself alone]
Piglialo sù, piglialo sù, Signor Monsu. What the deuce does it all mean?
[Seeing **SBRIGANI**]
Ah!

**SBRIGANI**
What is the matter, Sir? what ails you?

**MR. DE POURCEAUGNAC**
Everything I see seems injection.

**SBRIGANI**
How is that?

**MR. DE POURCEAUGNAC**
You can't think what has happened to me in that house where you took me.

**SBRIGANI**
No! What has happened?

**MR. DE POURCEAUGNAC**
I thought I should be well feasted there.

**SBRIGANI**
Well?

**MR. DE POURCEAUGNAC**
I leave you in this gentleman's hands. Doctors dressed in black. In a chair. Feel the pulse. In proof of what I say. He is mad. Two big, fat-faced fellows, with large-brimmed hats. Buon dì, buon dì. Six pantaloons. Ta, ra, ta, toi, ta, ra, ta, ta, toi. Allegramente, Monsu Pourceaugnac. Take, Sir; take, take. It is gentle, gentle, gentle. Piglialo sù, Signor Monsu; piglialo, piglialo sù. I never was so surfeited with absurdities in all my life.

**SBRIGANI**
What does it all mean?

**MR. DE POURCEAUGNAC**
It means, Sir, that this gentleman, with all his kissing and hugging, is a deceitful rascal, who has sent me to that house to play me some trick.

**SBRIGANI**
Is it possible?

**MR. DE POURCEAUGNAC**
It is, indeed. They were a dozen devils at my heels, and I had all the difficulty in the world to escape out of their clutches.

**SBRIGANI**
Just fancy how deceitful people's looks are; I should have taken him for the most affectionate friend you have. It is a wonder to me how there can exist such rascals in the world.

**MR. DE POURCEAUGNAC**
My imagination is full of it all; and it seems to me that I see everywhere a dozen injections threatening me.

**SBRIGANI**
This is really too bad! how treacherous and wicked people are!

**MR. DE POURCEAUGNAC**
Pray, tell me where Mr. Oronte lives. I should be glad to go there at once.

**SBRIGANI**
Ah! ah! you are of a loving disposition, I see; and you have heard that Mr. Oronte has a daughter?

**MR. DE POURCEAUGNAC**
Yes; I am come to marry her.

**SBRIGANI**
To ma ... to marry her?

**MR. DE POURCEAUGNAC**
Yes.

**SBRIGANI**
In wedlock?

**MR. DE POURCEAUGNAC**
How could it be otherwise?

**SBRIGANI**
Oh! it is another thing, and I beg your pardon.

**MR. DE POURCEAUGNAC**
What is it you mean?

**SBRIGANI**
Oh, nothing.

**MR. DE POURCEAUGNAC**
But, pray!

**SBRIGANI**
Nothing, I tell you. I spoke rather hastily.

**MR. DE POURCEAUGNAC**
I beg of you to tell me what it is.

**SBRIGANI**
No; it is not necessary.

**MR. DE POURCEAUGNAC**
Pray do.

**SBRIGANI**
No; I beg you to excuse me.

**MR. DE POURCEAUGNAC**
What! are you not one of my friends?

**SBRIGANI**
Yes, certainly; nobody more so.

**MR. DE POURCEAUGNAC**
Then you ought not to hide anything from me.

**SBRIGANI**
It is a thing in which a neighbour's honour is concerned.

**MR. DE POURCEAUGNAC**
That I may oblige you to treat me like a friend, here is a small ring I beg of you to keep for my sake.

**SBRIGANI**
Let me consider a little if I can in conscience do it.

[Goes away a small distance from **MR. DE POURCEAUGNAC**.

He is a man who looks after his own interests, who tries to provide for his daughter as advantageously as possible; and one should injure nobody. It is true that these things are no secret; but I shall be telling them to a man who knows nothing about it, and it is forbidden to talk scandal of one's neighbour. All this is true. On the other hand, however, here is a stranger they want to impose upon, who comes in all good faith to marry a girl he knows nothing about, and whom he has never seen. A gentleman all openheartedness, for whom I feel some inclination, who does me the honour of reckoning me his friend, puts his confidence in me, and gives me a ring to keep for his sake.
[To **MR. DE POURCEAUGNAC**]
Yes, I think that I can tell you how things are without wounding my conscience. But I must try to tell it all to you in the mildest way possible, and to spare people as much as I can. If I were to tell you that this girl leads a bad life, it would be going too far. I must find some milder term to explain myself. The word coquette does not come up to the mark; that of downright flirt seems to me to answer the purpose pretty well, and I can make use of it to tell you honestly what she is.

**MR. DE POURCEAUGNAC**
They want to make a fool of me then?

**SBRIGANI**
But it may not be so so bad as people think; and after all, there are men who set themselves above such things, and who do not think that their honour depends upon ...

**MR. DE POURCEAUGNAC**
I am your servant; I have no wish to adorn my person with such a head-dress, and the Pourceaugnacs are accustomed to walk with their heads free.

**SBRIGANI**
Here is the father.

**MR. DE POURCEAUGNAC**
Who? this old man?

**SBRIGANI**
Yes. Allow me to withdraw.

**ORONTE, MR. DE POURCEAUGNAC.**

**MR. DE POURCEAUGNAC**
Good morning, Sir; good morning.

**ORONTE**
Your servant, Sir; your servant.

**MR. DE POURCEAUGNAC**
You are Mr. Oronte; are you not?

**ORONTE**
Yes.

**MR. DE POURCEAUGNAC**
And I, Mr. de Pourceaugnac.

**ORONTE**
Ah, indeed!

**MR. DE POURCEAUGNAC**
Do you think, Mr. Oronte, that the people of Limoges are fools?

**ORONTE**
Do you think, Mr. de Pourceaugnac, that the people of Paris are asses?

**MR. DE POURCEAUGNAC**
Do you imagine, Mr. Oronte, that a man like me can be dying for a wife?

**ORONTE**
Do you imagine, Mr. de Pourceaugnac, that a daughter like mine can be dying for a husband?

**MR. DE POURCEAUGNAC, JULIA, ORONTE.**

**JULIA**

I have just been told, father, that Mr. de Pourceaugnac has come. Ah, there he is, no doubt; my heart tells me so. How handsome he is! How splendidly he holds himself. How pleased I am to have such a husband![11] Give me leave to kiss him and to show him....

**ORONTE**

Softly, daughter, softly.

**MR. DE POURCEAUGNAC** [Aside]

Heyday! At what a pace she goes, and how she takes fire!

**ORONTE**

I should very much like to know, Mr. de Pourceaugnac, for what reason you ...

**JULIA** [Approaches **MR. DE POURCEAUGNAC**, looks at him with a languishing look, and tries to take his hand]

How pleased I am to see you! And how impatient I am to ...

**ORONTE**

Hey! daughter, go away; will you?

**MR. DE POURCEAUGNAC** [Aside]

What a free and easy young damsel!

**ORONTE**

I should like to know what made you have the boldness to ...

[**JULIA** continues as above.

**MR. DE POURCEAUGNAC** [Aside]

By Jove!

**ORONTE** [To **JULIA**]

Again! What do you mean?

**JULIA**

May I not kiss the husband you have chosen for me?

**ORONTE**

No; go in.

**JULIA**

Allow me to look at him.

**ORONTE**

Go in, I tell you.

**JULIA**

I should like to stop here, if you please.

**ORONTE**
I will not suffer it. If you do not go in immediately, I ...

**JULIA**
Very well then, I will go in.

**ORONTE**
My daughter is a foolish girl who does not understand things.

**MR. DE POURCEAUGNAC** [Aside]
How taken she is with me!

**ORONTE** [To **JULIA**, who has stopped]
You won't go.

**JULIA**
When will yon marry me to this gentleman?

**ORONTE**
Never. You are not intended for him.

**JULIA**
I will have him, I will have him; you promised him to me.

**ORONTE**
If I promised him to you, I take my promise back again.

**MR. DE POURCEAUGNAC** [Aside]
She would fain eat me.

**JULIA**
Do what you will, we will be married in spite of everybody.

**ORONTE**
I shall know how to prevent it, I forewarn you. What madness has taken hold of her?


SCENE VII

**ORONTE, MR. DE POURCEAUGNAC.**

**MR. DE POURCEAUGNAC**
I say, our intended father-in-law, don't give yourself so much trouble; I have no intention of running away with your daughter; and your pretence won't take at all.

**ORONTE**
And yours will in no way succeed.

**MR. DE POURCEAUGNAC**
Did you think that Leonardo de Pourceaugnac is a man to buy a pig in a poke, and that he has not the sense to find out what goes on in the world, and to see if, in marrying, his honour is safe?

**ORONTE**
I do not know what you mean; but did you take into your head that a man of sixty-three years old has so little common sense, and so little consideration for his daughter, as to marry her to a man who has you know what, and who was put with a doctor to be cured?

**MR. DE POURCEAUGNAC**
This is a trick that was practised upon me, and there is nothing the matter with me.

**ORONTE**
The doctor told us so himself.

**MR. DE POURCEAUGNAC**
The doctor told a lie. I am a gentleman, and I will meet him sword in hand.

**ORONTE**
I know what I ought to believe, and you can no more impose upon me in this matter than about the debts you are bound to pay on your marriage day.

**MR. DE POURCEAUGNAC**
What debts?

**ORONTE**
It is of no use to affect ignorance. I have seen the Flemish merchant who with other creditors obtained a decision against you eight months ago.

**MR. DE POURCEAUGNAC**
What Flemish merchant? What creditors? What decision obtained against me?

**ORONTE**
You know perfectly well what I mean.


SCENE VIII

**MR. DR POURCEAUGNAC, ORONTE, LUCETTE.**

**LUCETTE** [Pretending to be a woman from Languedoc][12]
Oh, yèu be yur, be'e! an' I've avoun thee to làs, àrter all this yur tràepsin' vùrwurd an' backward. Cans thee now, yèu rascal; cans leuk me in the fae-as?

**MR. DE POURCEAUGNAC**
What is it this woman wants?

**LUCETTE**
What do I want o' thee, yèu villun! Thee's mak wise neet to know me, disn? an' thee disn turn rid nuther, èempodent oseburd that thee art! What! thee witn turn colour vur to leuk me in the fae-as! [To **ORONTE**]
I baent sàaf, Maister, nif'tis yèu that they do zay 'ee weeshth vur to marry wi' the darter o'? but 'owsomever I zwear to yèu, I be the weiv o' un, an' that zeben yur agone when 'ee was a travellin' drue Pézenas, he made out, we' 'iz falseness, that 'ee knowth zo wul 'ow vur act vur to come over my 'art, an' zo by one way or tother vur to git me vur to gèe unmy 'an vur to marry un.

**ORONTE**
Oh! oh!

**LUCETTE**
The rascal lef me dree yur àrterwurds, purtendin' that 'eed agot some bizness vur to deu in 'iz own country, an' ivur sinz I 'ant ayeard no news at all o' un; but when I wadn thinkin' nothin' 'tall 'bout 'ee, I yeard 'em say as 'ow 'ee was acomin' yur, into this yur town, vur to be amarried agee'an wi' another young ummun, that her father an' mother 'd apromised teu un athout knowin' nothin' 'ow that 'ee was amarried avore. Zo I starts toràcly, an' I be acome yur to this yur place so zeun's ivur I pausible keud, vur to staup this yur wicked marridge, an' vur to show op, avore all the wurld, the very wissest man that iver was.

**MR. DE POURCEAUGNAC**
What wonderful impudence!

**LUCETTE**
Eempurence! Baent yèu ashèe'amd o' yurzul vur to mak sport o' me, 'stid o' bein' abroke down wi' eenward feelins, that thee wicked 'art aurt vur to gee thee?

**MR. DE POURCEAUGNAC**
Do you mean to say that I am your husband?

**LUCETTE**
Villun! dis dare to zay tidn zo? Ah! thee's know wul 'nuf, wiss luck to me, that tis all zo treu's the Gauspel; an' I weesh to Heben twadn zo, an' that thee'ds alef me zo èenocent an' so quiet like eens I used to be, avore thy charms an' thy trumpery, bad luck, made me vur to 'sake it all! I nivur sheudn abin abrought down vur to be the pour weesh thing that I be now—vur to zee my man, cruel like, mak a laughin' sport of all the love that I've a 'ad vorn, an' lef me athout one beet o' pity, vur the mortal pàin I've abeared, 'bout the shee'amful way 'eev asàrd me.

**ORONTE**
Really, I feel quite ready to weep. Go! you are a wicked man!

**MR. DE POURCEAUGNAC, NÉRINE, LUCETTE, ORONTE.**

**NÉRINE** [Pretending to be from Picardy] [13]
Oh! Aa can stand nowt more; aa'm rait winded! Ah! good for nowt, thou's made me run well for it; thou'lt not 'scape me now. Joostice! Joostice! Aa forbid the weddin.
[To **ORONTE**]
He's my ain man, Mast-ther, and as sh'd joost loik to ave him stroong up, the precious hang-dog there.

**MR. DE POURCEAUGNAC**
Another!

**ORONTE**
What a devil of a man!

**LUCETTE**
An' what be yèu a-tullin' o', wai yur vurbèedin' an' yur 'àngin'? Thiki man's yo-ur ùzban, is ur?

**NÉRINE**
You're rait, Missis, an aa'm joost his woif.

**LUCETTE**
That's a lie then; 'tis me that's the rail weiv o' un; an eef 'ee ought vur to be a'ànged, why 'tis me that ought vur to 'ave it adeud.

**NÉRINE**
Me; aa can mak nowt o' that soort o' talk.

**LUCETTE**
I do tul 'ee 'ow that I be 'is weiv.

**NÉRINE**
His woif?

**LUCETTE**
Ees fie!

**NÉRINE**
Aa tell ye once more, that it's me at's joost that.

**LUCETTE**
An' I vows an' declares as 'ow tez me, my own zul.

**NÉRINE**
'Twere fowr yeer agone 'at he wed me.

**LUCETTE**
An' me, tez zeben yur sinz 'e teuk me vur 'iz weiv.

**NÉRINE**
Aa can proove aal 'at aa say.

**LUCETTE**
All my naibours knowth ut.

**NÉRINE**
Owr town can well witness to it.

**LUCETTE**
All Pézénas zeed us amarried.

**NÉRINE**
All Sin Quintin helpt at owr weddin'.

**LUCETTE**
Thur cant be nort more saafur.

**NÉRINE**
Nowt can be more sartin.

**LUCETTE** [To **MR. DE POURCEAUGNAC**]
Dis thee dare to zay òrt gin ut, yèu villun?

**NÉRINE** [To **MR. DE POURCEAUGNAC**]
Canst thou deny me, wicked man?

**MR. DE POURCEAUGNAC**
One is as true as the other.

**LUCETTE**
What èemperence! What, yèu rogue, yèu don't mind poor leedle Franky an' poor leedle Jinny—they that be the outcomin's o' our marridge?

**NÉRINE**
Joost look, there's cheek! What! thou's forgot yon poor cheel, owr little Maggy, 'at thou's lef me for a pledge o' thy faith?

**MR. DE POURCEAUGNAC**
What impudent jades!

**LUCETTE**
Yur Franky! Yur Jinny, come both o' ee, come both o' ee, come an' mak yur bad rascal of a father own to 'ow ee've asàrd all o' us.

**NÉRINE**

Coom hither, Maggy, maa cheel, coom heere quick, an' shame your fayther of th' impudence 'at he's gotten.


SCENE X

**MR. DE POURCEAUGNAC, ORONTE, LUCETTE, NÉRINE, SEVERAL CHILDREN.**

**CHILD**
Fayther! fayther! fayther!

**MR. DE POURCEAUGNAC**
Deuce take the little brats!

**LUCETTE**
What yèu, villun, artn thee fit to drap, vur to tak to yur chillurn arter jis farshin, an' to keep thee eyes vàs, 'feerd thee mids show lig a father teu 'em? Thee shetn git away vrom me, yèu scàulus oseburd! I'll volly thee ivery place, and cry op thee wickedness 'gin I've asàrd thee out, an' 'gin I've amade thee zwing. Rascal, I sheud like vur to mak thee zwing vor't, an' that I sheud.

**NÉRINE**
Wilt not bloosh to spaik yon words, an' to tak no thowt o'th kissin' o' yon poor cheel? Thou'lt not get clear o' ma claws; aa can tell thee! an spoit o' thy showin' thy teeth, aa'l mak thee know 'at aa'm thy woif, an' aa'l mak thee hang for it.

**CHILD**
Fayther! fayther! fayther!

**MR. DE POURCEAUGNAC**
Help! help! Where shall I run?

**ORONTE**
Go; you will do right to have him punished, and he richly deserves to be hanged.


SCENE XI

**SBRIGANI** [Alone]
Everything has been done according to my wish, and is succeeding admirably. We will so weary out our provincial that he will only be too thankful to leave the place.


SCENE XII

**MR. DE POURCEAUGNAC, SBRIGANI.**

**MR. DE POURCEAUGNAC**
Ah! I am murdered! What vexation! What a cursed town! Assassinated everywhere!

**SBRIGANI**
What is it, Sir? Has anything new happened?

**MR. DE POURCEAUGNAC**
Yes; it rains doctors and women in this country.

**SBRIGANI**
How is that?

**MR. DE POURCEAUGNAC**
Two jabbering jades have just been accusing me of being married to both of them, and have threatened me with justice.

**SBRIGANI**
This is a bad business, for in this country justice is terribly rigorous against that sort of crime.

**MR. DE POURCEAUGNAC**
Yes; but even if there should be information, citation, decree, and verdict obtained by surprise, default, and contumacy, I have still the alternative of a conflict of jurisdiction to gain time, and a resort to the means of nullity that will be found in the court case.

**SBRIGANI**
The very terms, and it is easy to see that you are in the profession, Sir.

**MR. DE POURCEAUGNAC**
I? Certainly not; I am a gentleman.[14]

**SBRIGANI**
But to speak as you do, you must have studied the law.

**MR. DE POURCEAUGNAC**
Not at all. It is only common sense which tells me that I shall always be admitted to be justified by facts, and that I could not be condemned upon a simple accusation, without witnesses, evidence, and confrontation with my adverse party.

**SBRIGANI**
This is more clever still.

**MR. DE POURCEAUGNAC**
These words come into my head without my knowledge.

**SBRIGANI**
It seems to me that the common sense of a gentleman may go so far as to understand what belongs to right and the order of justice, but not to know the very terms of chicane.

**MR. DE POURCEAUGNAC**
They are a few words I remember from reading novels.

**SBRIGANI**
Ah! I see.

**MR. DE POURCEAUGNAC**
To show you that I understand nothing of chicane, I beg of you to take me to a lawyer to have advice upon this affair.

**SBRIGANI**
Willingly. I will take you to two very clever men; but, first, I must tell you not to be surprised at their manner of speaking. They have contracted at the bar a certain habit of declaiming which looks like singing, and you would think all they tell you is nothing but music.

**MR. DE POURCEAUGNAC**
It does not matter how they speak, as long as they tell me what I wish to know!


SCENE XIII

**MR. DE POURCEAUGNAC, SBRIGANI, TWO LAWYERS, TWO ATTORNEYS, TWO SERGEANTS.**

**1ST LAWYER** [Drawling out his words]
Polygamy's a case, you find,
A case of hanging.

**2ND LAWYER** [Singing and speaking very fast]
Your deed
Is plain and clear,
And all the gear
Of wigs and law
Upon this flaw
One verdict bear.
Consult our authors,
Legislators and glossators,
Justinian, Papinian,
Ulpian and Tribonian,
Fernand, Rebuffe, Jean Imole,
Paul Castro, Julian Barthole, [15]
Jason, Aloyat, and Cujas
That mighty mind!
Polygamy's a case, you'll find,
A case of hanging.

**BALLET**, while the **2ND LAWYER** sings as before.

All nations civilised,
French, Dutch, and English,
Portuguese, Germans, Flemish,
Italians and Spanish,
By wisdom's sceptre swayed,
For this the self-same law have made.
The affair allows no doubt,
Polygamy's a case,
A case of hanging.

[**MR. DE POURCEAUGNAC**, irritated, drives them all away.

ACT III

SCENE I

**ÉRASTE, SBRIGANI.**

**SBRIGANI**
Yes; everything is succeeding splendidly; and as his knowledge of things is very shallow, and his understanding of the poorest, I put him in such a terrible fright at the severity of the law in this country, and at the preparations which were already set on foot to put him to death,[16] that he is determined to run away, and in order the better to escape from the people who, I have told him, are placed at the city gates to stop him, he has decided upon disguising himself as a woman.

**ÉRASTE**
How I should like to see him dressed up in that way!

**SBRIGANI**
Take care you carry out the farce properly; and whilst I go through my parts with him, you go and ...
[Whispers to him]
You understand, don't you?

**ÉRASTE**
Yes.

**SBRIGANI** [Whispers]
And when I have taken him where I mean....

**ÉRASTE**
All right.

**SBRIGANI** [Whispers]
And when the father has been forewarned by me....

**ÉRASTE**

Nothing could be better.

**SBRIGANI**

Here is our young lady. Go quickly; she must not see us together.


SCENE II

**MR. DE POURCEAUGNAC** [as a lady], **SBRIGANI**.

**SBRIGANI**

For my part, I don't think any one can know you, and you look exactly like a lady of birth.

**MR. DE POURCEAUGNAC**

I am so astonished that in this province the forms of justice should not be observed.

**SBRIGANI**

Yes; as I have already told you, they begin by hanging a man, and try him afterwards.

**MR. DE POURCEAUGNAC**

What unjust justice!

**SBRIGANI**

It is devilishly severe, particularly on this kind of crime.

**MR. DE POURCEAUGNAC**

Still, when one is innocent?

**SBRIGANI**

Ah me! They care little for that, and, besides, they have here a most intolerable hatred for the people of your province; and nothing gives them more pleasure than to hang a man from Limoges.[17]

**MR. DE POURCEAUGNAC**

What have the people from Limoges done to them?

**SBRIGANI**

How do I know? They are downright brutes, enemies to all the gentility and merit of other cities. For my part, I am in the greatest fear on your account, and I should never comfort myself if you were hanged.

**MR. DE POURCEAUGNAC**

It is not so much the fear of death that urges me to fly as the fact of being hanged, for it is a most degrading thing for a gentleman, and would ruin one's title of nobility.

**SBRIGANI**

You are right; after such a thing they would contest your right of bearing a title of nobility.[18] But, be careful, when I lead you by the hand, to walk like a woman, and to assume the manners and the language of a lady of quality.

**MR. DE POURCEAUGNAC**
Leave that to me; I have seen people of high standing in the world. The only thing that troubles me is that I have somewhat of a beard.

**SBRIGANI**
Oh! it's not worth mentioning. There are many women who have as much. Now, let us just see how you will behave yourself.

[**MR. DE POURCEAUGNAC** mimics a lady of rank.

Good.

**MR. DE POURCEAUGNAC**
Why, my carriage is not here! Where is my carriage? Gracious me! how wretched to have such attendants! Shall I have to wait all day in the street? Will not some one call my carriage for me?

**SBRIGANI**
Very good.

**MR. DE POURCEAUGNAC**
Soho! there, coachman. Little page! Ah! little rogue, what a whipping you will get by and by! Little page-boy! little page-boy! Where in the world is that page-boy? Will that little page never be found? Will nobody call that little page for me? Is my little page nowhere to be found?

**SBRIGANI**
Marvellous! But there is one thing that I see does not do. This hood is a little too thin; I must go and fetch you a thicker one, to hide your face better in case of any accident.

**MR. DE POURCEAUGNAC**
What shall I do in the meantime?

**SBRIGANI**
Wait for me here. I will be back in a moment; you have only to walk about.

[**MR. DE POURCEAUGNAC** walks forward and backward on the stage, mimicking the lady of rank.


SCENE III

**MR. DE POURCEAUGNAC, TWO SWISS.**

**1ST SWISS** [Without seeing **MR. DE POURCEAUGNAC**]

Come you, make haste, mein comrad, ve vill, both of us, go to ze market-place; to zee dis Porcegnac at de chustice, which him contemns to pe hung py de neck.

**2ND SWISS** [Without seeing **MR. DE POURCEAUGNAC**]
Ve moost hire one vindow to zee dis chustice.

**1ST SWISS**
Man says dat zey alreaty a great new gallow plant hafe, to hang dis Porcegnac to it.

**2ND SWISS**
It will pe, yes, a great pleazure to see dis Limossin hung.

**1ST SWISS**
Ja! to see him vaggle de feet up zere pefor all de peoples!

**2ND SWISS**
He pe one funny man, he pe; man says dat he married dree times hafe.

**1ST SWISS**
Ze room fellow! he vant dree wifes all to himself! one fery much pe quite enough for him.

**2ND SWISS** [Perceiving **MR. DE POURCEAUGNAC**]
Ah! goot tay, missy.

**1ST SWISS**
Vat do you zere all by self.

**MR. DE POURCEAUGNAC**
I am waiting for my servants, gentlemen.

**2ND SWISS**
You pe prooty, missy?

**MR. DE POURCEAUGNAC**
Gently, sirs.

**1ST SWISS**
Missy, vill you come and amuse you on de market-place? Ve will make you zee one little hanging fery prooty.

**MR. DE POURCEAUGNAC**
I am much obliged to you.

**2ND SWISS**
It is a Limossin chentleman vat will hung pe fery prootily at a great gallow.

**MR. DE POURCEAUGNAC**
I am not desirous to see it.

**1ST SWISS**
You hafe one much funny prest....

**MR. DE POURCEAUGNAC**
Ah! this is too much! and such odious things are not said to a woman of my position.

**2ND SWISS**
You go avay.

**1ST SWISS**
Me vill let not you.

**2ND SWISS**
Put I vill, I tell ye.

[Both lay hold of **MR. DE POURCEAUGNAC** roughly.

**1ST SWISS**
I vill not let you.

**2ND SWISS**
You hafe told one fery mooch lie.

**1ST SWISS**
You hafe told one lie yourself.

**MR. DE POURCEAUGNAC**
Help! help! police!


SCENE IV

**MR. DE POURCEAUGNAC, THREE POLICE OFFICERS, TWO SWISS.**

**OFFICER**
What is it? what is the meaning of this violence? and what are you doing to this lady? Be off at once, unless you wish to be put in prison.

**1ST SWISS**
Goot, you gone, you vill not hafe her.

**2ND SWISS**
Goot, you gone too, you vill not hafe her also.

**MR. DE POURCEAUGNAC, THREE POLICE OFFICERS.**

**MR. DE POURCEAUGNAC**
I am much obliged to you, Sir, for saving me from those insolent fellows.

**OFFICER**
Oh! oh! This is a face which is deucedly like that which was described to me.

**MR. DE POURCEAUGNAC**
It is not I, I assure you.

**OFFICER**
Oh! oh! what does this mean?

**MR. DE POURCEAUGNAC**
I don't know.

**OFFICER**
What is it, then, that makes you say that?

**MR. DE POURCEAUGNAC**
Nothing.

**OFFICER**
This manner of speaking is somewhat ambiguous, and you are my prisoner.

**MR. DE POURCEAUGNAC**
O, Sir, I pray!

**OFFICER**
No, no; to judge by your appearance and your manner of speaking, you must be that Mr. de Pourceaugnac we are looking for, although you are disguised in this manner, and you must come to prison at once.

**MR. DE POURCEAUGNAC**
Alas!

SCENE VI

**MR. DE POURCEAUGNAC, SBRIGANI, THREE POLICE OFFICERS.**

**SBRIGANI** [To **MR. DE POURCEAUGNAC**]
Heavens! what does this mean?

**MR. DE POURCEAUGNAC**
They have discovered who I am.

**OFFICER**
Yes, yes; I am delighted about it.

**SBRIGANI** [To the **OFFICER**]
Ah, Sir! for my sake! do not take him to prison; you know that we have been friends a long while.

**OFFICER**
I cannot help it.

**SBRIGANI**
You are a man to hear reason. Is there no way of adjusting this matter with the help of a few pistoles?

**OFFICER** [To his **SUBORDINATES**]
Go farther back.


SCENE VII

**MR. DE POURCEAUGNAC, SBRIGANI, A POLICE OFFICER.**

**SBRIGANI** [To **MR. DE POURCEAUGNAC**]
You must give him some money for him to let you go. Be quick.

**MR. DE POURCEAUGNAC** [Giving some money to **SBRIGANI**]
Ah! cursed place.

**SBRIGANI**
Here, Sir.

**OFFICER**
How much is there?

**SBRIGANI**
One, two, three, four, five, six, seven, eight, nine, ten.

**OFFICER**
No; I have express orders.

**SBRIGANI** [To the **OFFICER**, who is going]
Pray wait.
[To **MR. DE POURCEAUGNAC**]
Be quick, give him as much again.

**MR. DE POURCEAUGNAC**

But ...

**SBRIGANI**
Be quick, I tell you; don't waste time; you would be happy, would you not, if you were hanged?

**MR. DE POURCEAUGNAC**
Ah!

[Gives more money to **SBRIGANI**.

**SBRIGANI** [To the **OFFICER**]
Here, Sir.

**OFFICER** [To **SBRIGANI**]
I must go off with him, for I should not be in safety here after this. Leave him to me, and don't stir from this place.

**SBRIGANI**
I beg of you to take the utmost care of him.

**OFFICER**
I promise you not to leave him one moment till I see him safe.

**MR. DE POURCEAUGNAC** [To **SBRIGANI**]
Farewell! This is the first honest man I have found in this town.

SCENE VIII

**ORONTE, SBRIGANI.**

**SBRIGANI** [Affecting not to see **ORONTE**]
Ah! What a strange adventure! What terrible news for a father! Poor Oronte, how much I pity you! What will you say? How will you ever be able to bear with such a misfortune?

**ORONTE**
What is it? Of what misfortune do you speak?

**SBRIGANI**
Ah, Sir! This wretch of a Limousin has run away with your daughter!

**ORONTE**
Run away with my daughter!

**SBRIGANI**
Yes; she became so infatuated with him that she has left you to follow him. It is said that he has a charm to make all women fall in love with him.

**ORONTE**

Quick! Justice! Let the police be set after them!

**ORONTE, ÉRASTE, JULIA, SBRIGANI.**

**ÉRASTE** [To **JULIA**]

Come along; you shall come in spite of yourself. I will put you in your father's hands. Sir, here is your daughter, whom I had to take by force from the man with whom she was running away; it is not for her sake that I did it, but entirely for yours. For, after such conduct, I ought to despise her, and it is enough to cure me altogether of my love.

**ORONTE**

Ah! infamous girl that you are!

**ÉRASTE** [To **JULIA**]

How could you treat me in that way, after all the proofs of affection I have given you? I do not blame you for being obedient to your father's will; he is wise and judicious in all he does; and I do not complain of him for having preferred another to me. They told him that that other man was richer than I by four or five thousand crowns, and four or five thousand crowns are a good round sum, and are enough to make a gentleman break his word; but that you should forget in a moment all the love I had for you, suffer yourself to fall madly in love with the first new-comer, and shamefully follow him; without the consent of your father, after all the crimes that were charged upon him! It is what all the world will condemn, and what my heart can never cease to reproach you with.

**JULIA**

Well, yes; I fell in love with him, and I wanted to follow him, since my father had chosen him to be my husband. Whatever you may say, he is a very honest man, and all the crimes they accuse him of are so many detestable falsehoods.

**ORONTE**

Be silent; you are an impertinent hussy, and I know better than you.

**JULIA**

They are some tricks they have played him, and…

[Showing **ÉRASTE**.

—it is he himself, no doubt, who managed it all, to disgust you with him.

**ÉRASTE**

What! I should be capable of such a thing?

**JULIA**

Yes, you.

**ORONTE**
Be silent, I tell you. You are a silly girl.

**ÉRASTE**
You need not think that I have any wish to prevent the match, and that it is because I love you that I hastened to rescue you. I have already told you that it is only because of the regard I have for your father. I could not bear to see an honourable man exposed to the shame of all the gossip that would be occasioned by such an action.

**ORONTE**
I am truly and sincerely obliged to you, Sir.

**ÉRASTE**
Farewell, Sir! I had the greatest desire to enter into your family; I did everything to deserve such an honour; but I have been unfortunate, and you did not judge me worthy of that honour. It will not prevent me from retaining towards you all those feelings of esteem and regard which your person demands; and although I cannot be your son-in-law, I shall always be at your service.

**ORONTE**
Stay. Your behaviour touches my heart, and I give you my daughter in marriage.

**JULIA**
I won't have any other husband than Mr. de Pourceaugnac.

**ORONTE**
And I will have you marry Éraste at once.

**JULIA**
No; I will not.

**ORONTE**
I shall give it you about the ears.

**ÉRASTE**
No, no, Sir; don't use violence towards her, I pray you.

**ORONTE**
I will have her obey me, and I will show her that I am the master.

**ÉRASTE**
Do you not see how fast in love she is with that man; and would you have me possess the body while another has the heart?

**ORONTE**
He has thrown some charm upon her. You may be sure that she will change before long. Give me your hand. Come.

**JULIA**
No!

**ORONTE**
Ah! What, rebellion! Your hand, I tell you, at once. Ah!

**ÉRASTE**
Do not think that it is because of my love for you that I agree to marry you; it is your father only I am in love with, and it is him whom I marry.

**ORONTE**
I am truly obliged to you, and I add ten thousand crowns to my daughter's portion. Quick; a notary to draw up the contract.

**ÉRASTE**
In the meanwhile, let us enjoy the pleasures of the season, and fetch in those masks whom the report of Mr. de Pourceaugnac's wedding has attracted hither.

SCENE X

**A BALLET**

*FOOTNOTES:*

*1. Pourceaugnac equals pourceau, "a young pig," plus the local ending -gnac.*

*2. Compare the "royal cautery" in 'The Flying Doctor'.*

*3. Sbrigani and Nérine are merely the conventional rogues of the stage. Compare Mascarille, Scapin.*

*4. Compare act ii. scene xii.*

*5. The Neapolitans had no great reputation for sincerity.*

*6. Mode de la cour pour la campagne.*

*7. Consul in the south equalled chevin in the north. Both words are obsolete in this sense.*

*8Ma croix de par Dieu, "my Christ-cross-row," or "Criss-cross-row," in old and provincial English.*

*9. Translation*
*THE TWO PHYSICIANS.*
*Good day, good day, good day!*

*Yield not yourself a prey*
*To melancholy sway.*
*We'll make you laugh, I trow,*
*With songs harmonious, gay.*
*Unto us your cure is dear,*
*For that alone we're here.*
*Good day, good day, good day!*

*1ST PHYSICIAN.*
*Nought else is madness true*
*Save melancholy blue.*
*Not lost is he,*
*Though sick he be,*
*Who sips of mirth the dew.*
*Nought else is madness true*
*Save melancholy blue.*

*2ND PHYSICIAN.*
*Up then! sing loud, and dance and play,*
*"Better still I'd do!" you say.*
*Delirium's nigh—if you must pine,*
*Take first some wine;*
*And sometimes, too, take your tabàc*
*Right joyfully, Monsu Pourceaugnac.*

*10. Take it, take it. Sir; it will do you no harm, &c.*

*11. See act i, scene iii.*

*12. Somerset dialect is employed here.*

*13. Lowland Scotch is employed here.*

*14. Compare act i. scene v.*

*15. The French forms have been retained for the sake of the rhyme.*

*16. Bigamists were really put to death.*

*17. Molière seems to have had a grudge against Limoges. Compare act i. scene i.*

*18. Footnote: Noblemen were beheaded.*

Jean-Baptiste Poquelin is better known to us by his stage name of Molière. He was born in Paris, to a prosperous well-to-do family, the son of Jean Poquelin and Marie Cressé, on 15th January 1622.

It is said that a maid, seeing him for the first time shrieked, "Le nez!", a reference to the infant's large nose. The name stuck as a family nickname from that time. At ten his mother died and his relationship with his father seems to have been lukewarm at best.

It is probable that his education started with studies in a Parisian elementary school. This was followed with his enrolment in the prestigious Jesuit Collège de Clermont, where he completed his studies in a strict academic environment but also first sampled life on the stage.

In 1631, his father purchased from the court of Louis XIII the posts of "valet de chambre ordinaire et tapissier du Roi" ("valet of the King's chamber and keeper of carpets and upholstery").

Molière assumed his father's posts in 1641. The benefits included only three months' work per annum for which he was paid 300 livres and also provided a number of lucrative contracts.

To increase the spectrum of his skills Molière also studied as a provincial lawyer around 1642, probably in Orléans, but it is not recorded if he ever qualified. Up to this date he had followed his father's plans for a career and they had served him well; he seemed destined for a career in office.

However, in June 1643, when he was 21, Molière abandoned this path for his first love; a career on the stage. He partnered with the actress Madeleine Béjart, to found the Illustre Théâtre at a cost of 630 livres.

Unfortunately, despite their enthusiasm, effort and ambition the troupe went bankrupt in 1645. Molière, now in charge, due to both his acting prowess and his legal training, had run up debts, mainly for the rent of the theatre, of 2000 livres. Molière was thrown into prison. Historians differ as to who paid the debts but after a 24-hour stint in jail Molière returned to the acting circuit.

It was at this time that he began to use the pseudonym Molière. It may also have been to spare his father the shame of having an actor in the family; a lowly profession for his status in society.

Molière and Madeleine now began with a new group of actors and spent the next dozen years touring the provincial circuit. The company slowly gained in success. Molière was also writing much of what they acted. Sadly only a few plays survive from this period among them 'The Bungler' and 'The Doctor in Love'. They represent though a distinct move away from the Italian improvisational Commedia dell'arte and highlight his use of mockery.

Armand, Prince of Conti, the governor of Languedoc, now also became his patron in return the company was named after him. Sadly for Molière the friendship later ended when Conti, having contracted syphilis from a courtesan, turned towards religion and joined Molière's enemies in the Parti des Dévots and the Compagnie de Saint Sacrement.

Molière's' journey back to the sacred land of Parisian theatres was slow. However by 1658 he performed in front of the King at the Louvre (then a theatre for hire) in Corneille's tragedy 'Nicomède' and in the farce 'Le Docteur Amoureux' (The Doctor in Love) with some success. He was awarded the title of Troupe de Monsieur (Monsieur being the honorific for the king's brother Philippe I, Duke of

Orléans). With the help of Monsieur, his company was allowed to share the theatre in the large hall of the Petit-Bourbon with the famous Italian Commedia dell'arte company of Tiberio Fiorillo. The companies performed in the theatre on alternate nights.

The premiere of Molière's 'Les Précieuses Ridicules' (The Affected Young Ladies) took place at the Petit-Bourbon on 18th November 1659. It was the first of Molière's many attempts to satirize certain societal mannerisms and affectations then common in France. It won Molière the attention and the criticism of many, but alas not a large audience. He then asked Fiorillo to teach him the techniques of Commedia dell'arte. His 1660 play 'Sganarelle, ou Le Cocu imaginaire' (The Imaginary Cuckold) seems to be a tribute both to Commedia dell'arte and to his teacher.

Despite his own preference for tragedy, Molière became famous for these farces, which were generally in one act and performed after the tragedy. Some of these farces were only partly written and performed in the style of Commedia dell'arte with improvisation over a sketched out plot. He also wrote two comedies in verse, but these were less successful.

In 1660 the Petit-Bourbon was demolished to make way for the expansion of the Louvre. Molière's company decamped to the abandoned theatre in the Palais-Royal which was in the process of being refurbished. The company opened there on 20th January 1661. In order to please his patron, Monsieur, who was so enthralled with the arts that he was soon excluded from state affairs, Molière wrote and played 'Dom Garcie de Navarre ou Le Prince jaloux' (The Jealous Prince, 4th February 1661), a heroic comedy derived from a work of Cicognini's. Two other comedies of the same year were the successful 'L'École des maris' (The School for Husbands) and 'Les Fâcheux', (The Mad also known as The Bores) subtitled Comédie faite pour les divertissements du Roi (a comedy for the King's amusements) as it was performed during a series of parties that Nicolas Fouquet gave in honor of the king. These entertainments led to the arrest of Fouquet for wasting public money. He was sentenced to life imprisonment.

In parallel with 'Les Fâcheux', Molière introduced the comédies-ballets. These ballets were a transitional form of dance performance between the court ballets of Louis XIV and the art of professional theatre which was developing rapidly with the use of the proscenium stage. The comédies-ballets developed by chance when Molière was enlisted to mount both a play and a ballet in the honor of Louis XIV and found that he did not have a large enough cast to meet the needs of both. Cleverly Molière decided to combine the ballet and the play to achieve his goals. The gamble paid off handsomely. Molière was asked to produce twelve more comédies-ballets before his death. During these Molière collaborated with Pierre Beauchamp. Beauchamp codified the five balletic positions of the feet and arms and was partly responsible for the creation of the Beauchamp-Feuillet dance notation. He also collaborated with Jean-Baptiste Lully, a dancer, choreographer, and composer, whose reign at the Paris Opéra ran for fifteen years. Under Molière's command, ballet and opera became professional arts unto themselves. The comédies-ballets closely integrated dance with music and the action of the play and the style of continuity distinctly separated these performances from the court ballets of the time; additionally, the comédies-ballets demanded that both the dancers and the actors play an important role in advancing the story. Intriguingly Louis XIV played the part of an Egyptian in 'Le Mariage forcé' (1664) and also appeared as Neptune and Apollo in his retirement performance of 'Les Amants magnifiques' (1670).

On 20th February 1662 Molière married Armande Béjart, whom he believed to be the sister of Madeleine. The same year he premiered 'L'École des Femmes' (The School for Wives), widely regarded as a masterpiece. It poked fun at the limited education given to daughters of rich families and reflected on Molière's own marriage. It attracted a lot of outraged criticism and ignited the protest called the "Quarrel of L'École des femmes". Molière responded with two works: 'La Critique de "L'École des femmes"', in which he imagined the audience of the previous work attending it. It mocks them by presenting them at dinner after watching the play; it addresses all the criticism raised about the piece by presenting the critics' arguments and then dismissing them. This was the so-called Guerre comique (War of Comedy), in which the opposite side was taken by writers like Donneau de Visé, Edmé Boursault, and Montfleury.

But more serious opposition was brewing, focusing on Molière's politics and his personal life. Some in French high society protested against Molière's excessive realism and irreverence, which were causing some embarrassment. Despite this the King expressed support for him. Molière was granted a pension and the King agreed to be the godfather of Molière's first son.

Molière's friendship with Jean-Baptiste Lully influenced him towards writing his 'Le Mariage forcé' and 'La Princesse d'Élide', written for royal divertissements at the Palace of Versailles.

'Tartuffe, ou L'Imposteur' was also performed at Versailles, in 1664, and created the greatest scandal of Molière's artistic career. Its depiction of the hypocrisy of the dominant classes was taken as an outrage and violently contested. It also aroused the wrath of the Jansenists (a Catholic theological movement, that emphasized original sin, human depravity, the necessity of divine grace, and predestination). The play was banned.

Molière was always careful not to attack the monarchy in any way. He had won a position as one of the king's favourites and enjoyed his protection from the attacks of the court. When the King suggested that Molière suspend performances of 'Tartuffe', Molière complied and quickly wrote 'Dom Juan ou le Festin de Pierre' (Don Juan, or, The Stone Banquet) to replace it. The story is of an atheist who becomes a religious hypocrite and is punished by God. But this too fell foul and was quickly suspended. The King, still keen to protect Molière became the new official sponsor of Molière's troupe.

With music by Lully, Molière presented 'Love Doctor or Medical Love'. The work was given "par ordre du Roi" (by order of the King) and was received much more warmly than its predecessors.

In 1666, 'Le Misanthrope' was produced. Molière's masterpiece. Although brimming with moral content it was little appreciated at the time and a commercial flop, forcing Molière to immediately write 'The Doctor Despite Himself', a satire against the official sciences. This was a success despite a moral treatise by the Prince of Conti, criticizing the theater in general and Molière in particular.

After the Mélicerte and the Pastorale comique, he tried again to perform a revised 'Tartuffe' in 1667, this time with the name of Panulphe or L'Imposteur. As soon as the King left Paris for a tour, the play was banned. The King finally imposed respect for 'Tartuffe' some years later, when he gained more power over the clergy.

Molière, now ill, wrote at a slower pace. 'Le Sicilien ou L'Amour peintre' (The Sicilian, or Love the Painter) was written for festivities at the castle of Saint-Germain-en-Laye, and was followed in 1668 by 'Amphitryon'.

'George Dandin, ou Le mari confondu' (The Confounded Husband) was little appreciated, but success returned with 'L'Avare' (The Miser), now very well known.

With Lully he again used music for 'Monsieur de Pourceaugnac', for 'Les Amants magnifiques' (The Magnificent Lovers), and finally for 'Le Bourgeois gentilhomme' (The Middle-Class Gentleman), another of his masterpieces. The collaboration with Lully ended with a tragédie et ballet, 'Psyché', written in collaboration with Pierre Corneille and Philippe Quinault.

In 1672, Madeleine Béjart died. It was a heavy blow to Molière who was already in declining health himself. However, he continued to write and his plays were eagerly awaited and performed. 'Les Fourberies de Scapin' (The Impostures of Scapin), a farce and a comedy in five acts was successful. The following play, 'La Comtesse d'Escarbagnas' (The Countess of Escarbagnas), is thought of as a lesser works.

'Les Femmes savantes' (The Learned Ladies) of 1672 is accepted as another masterpieces. It was born from the termination of the legal use of music in theater, (Lully had patented the opera in France and taken the best singers for his own works), so Molière returned to his traditional genre. It was a great success.

Molière suffered from pulmonary tuberculosis. One of the most famous moments in Molière's life was his last: he collapsed on stage in a fit of coughing and haemorrhaging while performing in the last play he'd written, in which, ironically, he was playing the hypochondriac Argan, in 'The Imaginary Invalid'.

Molière insisted on completing his performance.

Afterwards he collapsed again with another, larger haemorrhage and was taken home. Priests were sent for to administer the last rites. Two priests refused to visit. A third arrived too late. On 17th February 1673, Jean-Baptiste Poquelin, forever to be known as Molière, was pronounced dead in Paris. He was 51.

Under French law at the time, actors were forbidden to be buried in sacred ground. Molière's widow asked the King if Molière could be granted a normal funeral at night. The King agreed.

In his life Molière divided opinion. He was adored by the court and Parisians but loathed and reviled by moralists and the Catholic Church.

In 1792 his remains were brought to the museum of French monuments. In 1817 they were transferred to Père Lachaise Cemetery in Paris, close to those of La Fontaine.

In his 14 years in Paris, Molière singlehandedly wrote 31 of the 85 plays performed on his stage. His immensely popular legacy includes comedies, farces, tragicomedies and comédie-ballets.


Molière – A Concise Bibliography

Le Médecin Volant (1645)—The Flying Doctor
La Jalousie du Barbouillé (1650)—The Jealousy of le Barbouillé
L'Étourdi, ou le Contre-Temps(1653)—The Scatterbrain or The Bungler
L'Étourdi ou les Contretemps (1655)—The Blunderer, or, the Counterplots

Le Dépit Amoureux (16 December 1656)—The Love-Tiff
Le Docteur Amoureux (1658), 1st play performed by Molière's troupe (now lost)—The Doctor in Love
Les Précieuses Ridicules (1659)—The Affected Young Ladies
Sganarelle ou Le Cocu Imaginaire (1660)— Sganarelle or, The Self-Deceived Husband aka The Imaginary Cuckold
Dom Garcie de Navarre ou Le Prince Jaloux (1661)—Don Garcia of Navarre or the Jealous Prince
L'École des Maris (1661)—The School for Husbands
Les Fâcheux (17 August 1661)—The Mad aka The Bores
L'École des Femmes (1662; adapted into The Amorous Flea, 1964)—The School for Wives
La Jalousie du Gros-René (1663)—The Jealousy of Gros-René
La Critique de l'école des Femmes (1663)—Critique of the School for Wives
L'Impromptu de Versailles (1663)—The Versailles Impromptu
Le Mariage Forcé (1664)—The Forced Marriage
Gros-René, Petit Enfant (1664; now lost)—Gros-René, Small Child
La Princesse d'Élide (1664)—The Princess of Elid
Tartuffe ou L'Imposteur (1664)—Tartuffe, or, the Impostor
Dom Juan ou Le Festin de Pierre (1665)—Don Juan, or, The Stone Banquet (aka The Stone Guest, The Feast with the Statue)
L'Amour médecin (1665)—Love Is the Doctor aka Medical Love
Le Misanthrope ou L'Atrabilaire Amoureux (1666)—The Misanthrope, or, the Cantankerous Lover
Le Médecin Malgré Lui (1666)—The Physican in Spite of Himself aka A Doctor Despite Himself
Mélicerte (1666)
Pastorale Comique (1667)—Comic Pastoral
Le Sicilien ou L'Amour Peintre (1667)—The Sicilian, or Love the Painter
Amphitryon (1668)
George Dandin ou Le Mari Confondu (1668)—George Dandin, or, the Abashed Husband
L'Avare ou L'École du Mensonge (1668)—The Miser, or, the School for Lies
Monsieur de Pourceaugnac (1669)
Les Amants Magnifiques (1670)—The Magnificent Lovers
Le Bourgeois Gentilhomme (1670)—The Middle-Class Gentleman aka The Shopkeeper Turned Gentleman
Psyché (1671)—Psyche
Les Fourberies de Scapin (1671)—The Impostures of Scapin
La Comtesse d'Escarbagnas (1671)—The Countess of Escarbagnas
Les Femmes Savantes (1672)—The Learned Ladies aka The Learned Women
Le Malade Imaginaire (1673)—The Imaginary Invalid

www.ingramcontent.com/pod-product-compliance
Lightning Source LLC
Chambersburg PA
CBHW060052050426
42448CB00011B/2416